LUCKY HARES
AND
ITCHY BEARS

POEMS BY SUSAN EWING
ILLUSTRATIONS BY EVON ZERBETZ

ALASKA NORTHWEST BOOKS™
Anchorage ▪ Portland

OCTOPUS

You can call him egghead,
He really would be charmed.

He's quite a bright invertebrate,
Not dangerous—though armed.

Imagine being hugged by
First those tentacles, then these,

Eight rubbery arms around your waist
To give you such a squeeze.

His suction cups get puckered
And clamp upon your skin,

Then when you try to peel him off,
Oh, where do you begin?

SEA OTTER

Imagine munching urchins
While floating on your back
And smashing clams upon your chest—
It's **WHAM**, and then **CUH-RACK!**

For otter it's not awkward
To snack or snooze afloat,
He bobs upon the ocean waves
Just like a furry boat.

And just like boats have anchors
To stay right where they are,
Otter
   wraps
      himself
         in kelp
            To keep from drifting far.

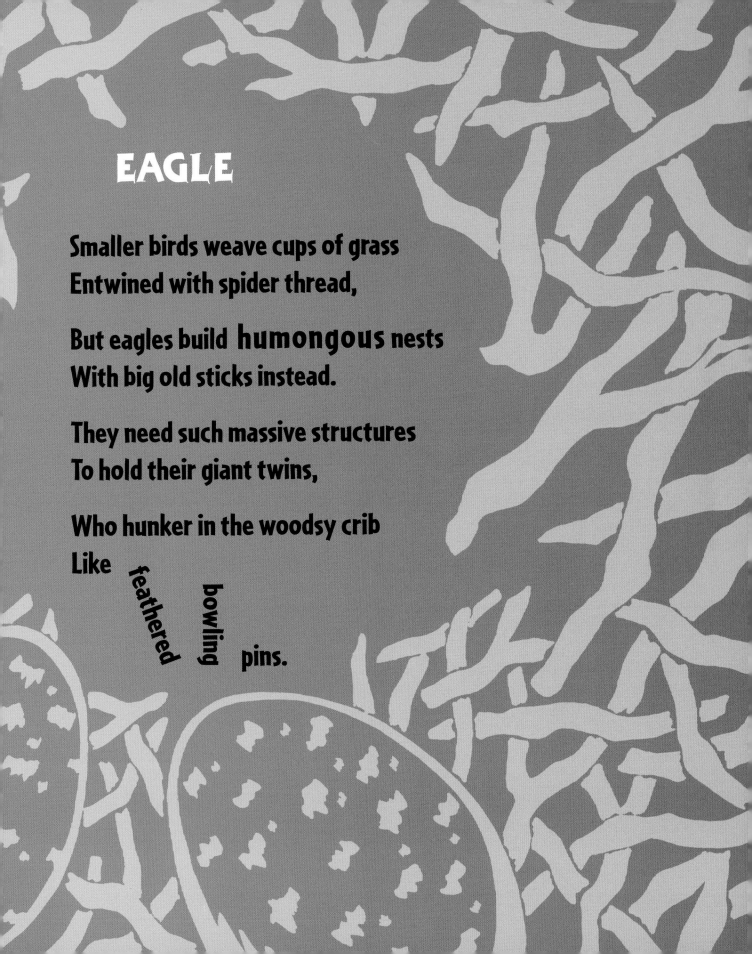

EAGLE

Smaller birds weave cups of grass
Entwined with spider thread,

But eagles build **humongous** nests
With big old sticks instead.

They need such massive structures
To hold their giant twins,

Who hunker in the woodsy crib
Like feathered bowling pins.

FLYING SQUIRREL

Jump. *Wheee! She glides toward the ground.*

In flying squirrel style, she makes not a sound.

Then over the floor of the forest she skitters
Keeping an eye out for other night critters.

Hiding from owl—to avoid any scuffle—
She snuffles around in the ground for a truffle.

By dawn, yawning squirrel knows it's time for a rest
So she scampers on back to her cozy twig nest.

SNOWSHOE HARE

Oh my gosh, I've **got** to run–
Lynx is here to spoil the fun.

My feet are built to tread the snow,
But so are hers, you ought to know.

Oh no, she's gaining–a spurt of speed–
Am I to be her bunny feed?!

Z i g ,   z a g ,   d a s h–I'm past her,
Today *my* furry feet are faster!

I never ever want to lose
My lucky little running shoes.

MOOSE

You know it's not polite to stare
Still, moose can give you pause.

Those skinny legs! Those droopy ears!
How does he blow that schnozz?

But with his legs he's happy,
With his nose content.

Moose can walk forever
And smell the smallest scent.

He can wade in water
Above his knobby knees.

And if a leaf gets up his snoot . . .
Watch out! He's gonna SNEEZE!

HUMPBACK WHALE

A humpback leaps at any chance
To prove you don't need feet to dance–

Lunging with dramatic flair
Flinging clear into the air.

His flippers flap like whaley wings
Or like a maestro's motionings.

When–s $p^{o^{o^{o}}o}$sh–he dives without a trace
The ocean seems a quiet place.

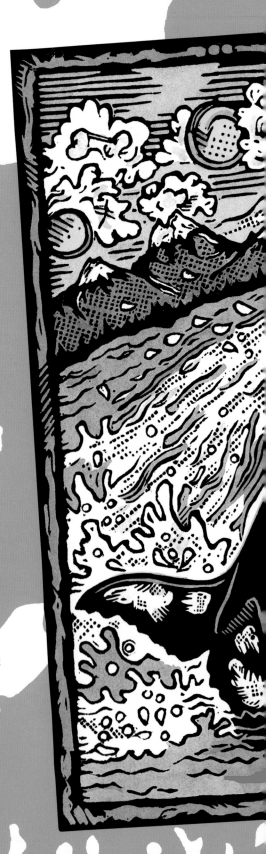

BEAR

Discovering the tracks of bear
Can bring on quite a little scare.

You hope you don't—you hope you do—
See the bears ahead of you.

If you're careful, if you wish,
You'll find your brown bears eating fish.

Or ((SCRATCHING)) up against a tree,
Itching bear behinds with glee.

SALMON

When you spy a salmon
Swimming hard upstream,
She's seen more sights and had more frights
Than you could ever dream.

She moved from stream to ocean
When she was just a kid,
She's had to outrun orcas
She's dined on squiggly squid.

Now with a school of siblings
All fighting to get home,
She shimmies past a fishing bear
And leaps through falls and foam.

Nose straight into the current
She finds the place she knows.
Where she was born, she lays her eggs,
And on the story goes.

FROG

Froggy Boy, I have to ask ya,
Whatcha doin' in Alaska?

How do you survive the chill?
A heat lamp? Or perhaps a pill?

Oh! Snowy blanket tucks you in
From froggy feet to froggy chin.

And so you're quite content to doze
While all the world around is froze.

When spring days come, you groggy frogs
Crawl out from under soggy bogs.

It's time to wake from winter's sleep—
Uh-ribbet croak uh-

reep-

reep-

reep!

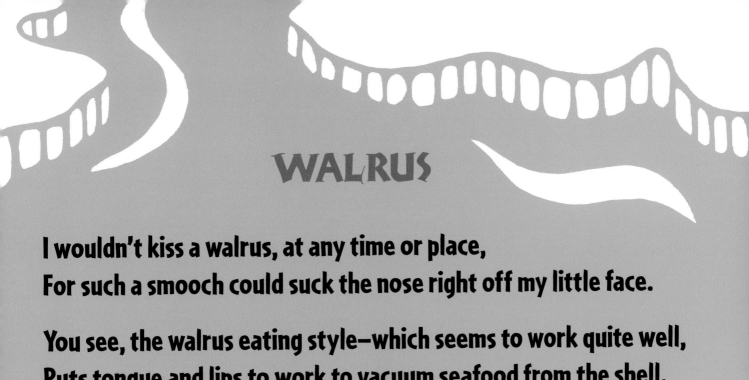

WALRUS

I wouldn't kiss a walrus, at any time or place,
For such a smooch could suck the nose right off my little face.

You see, the walrus eating style—which seems to work quite well,
Puts tongue and lips to work to vacuum seafood from the shell.

Upside-down, they feel around for food with whiskered muzzle,
Nosing clams out of the sand, giving crabs a nuzzle.

Tusks are used for other tasks, but if I may be honest,
If I had teeth like that I'd call my brother's orthodontist.

RAVEN

WHOOSH–wind flows over raven's wing,
He flaps with feathered grace.
This shiny trickster flies for fun,
Not just to get someplace.

He *KULKS* quite conversationally
While swooping to and fro,
I listen up in case he *KROOKS*
A word that I might know.

In stories ravens used to talk,
I'm thinking they still do–
Just listen to this bird rave on
About his bird's-eye view.

CARIBOU

Yoo-hoo, Caribou, where are you going now?
Is migration like vacation? Excuse me? Mrs. Cow?

Spend the summer over here, the winter over there,
Have your baby somewhere else, then migrate off elsewhere.

You give your tiny calf about an hour to get ready,
But just in time to move again, that baby's walking steady.

Your little girl is lucky to be born a caribou,
For unlike female deer or moose, she will grow antlers too!

WOLF

Nose licking, tails wagging, paws pawing ears,
It's family reunion when Big Wolf appears.

Now father and mother and pups in a pack
Set off together to sniff breeze and track.

Pausing a moment in milky moonlight,
They wonder who else is out hunting tonight.

HOWWWWIIIIIIOOOOOO they sing out,
then let silence *fall*,
To listen for neighbors returning the call.

DRAGONFLY

Mosquito never had a chance
When dragonfly asked, *Shall we dance?*

She waltzed mosquito north and south—
He jitterbugged into her mouth.

Gotcha! grinned sly dragonfly,
Hovering lightly in the sky.

Then with a *thrumm* she sped away,
"Who else would like to dance today?"